MW01601961

PRENTICE HALL

DIGGING FOR
ANSWERS

PEARSON

Prentice
Hall

Boston, Massachusetts
Upper Saddle River, New Jersey

**Copyright © 2007 by Pearson Education, Inc., publishing as Prentice Hall,
Boston, Massachusetts 02116**. All rights reserved. Printed in the United States of
America. This publication is protected by copyright, and permission should be obtained
from the publisher prior to any prohibited reproduction, storage in a retrieval system,
or transmission in any form or by any means, electronic, mechanical, photocopying,
recording, or likewise. For information regarding permission(s), write to: Rights and
Permissions Department, One Lake Street, Upper Saddle River, New Jersey 07458.

Pearson Prentice Hall™ is a trademark of Pearson Education, Inc.

Pearson® is a registered trademark of Pearson plc.

Prentice Hall® is a registered trademark of Pearson Education, Inc.

ISBN-13: 978-0-13-363632-1
ISBN-10: 0-13-363632-1
4 V088 11

PRENTICE HALL DISCOVERIES

Digging for Answers

What is important to know?

Table of Contents

Searching for Pompeii

Vesuvius is the name of an **immense** mountain in southern Italy. Vesuvius is not an ordinary mountain. It is a volcano. This is an opening in the Earth's crust through which melted rock, called lava, and gases sometimes erupt. Long periods of time can pass between eruptions. This was true of Vesuvius.

In the year 79, no one living near Vesuvius knew that it was a volcano. Nearly 20,000 people lived in a grand city in its shadow. That city was Pompeii. Today, we know that Pompeii was built on lava from Vesuvius eruptions in prehistoric times. We know many other important and interesting things about the ancient city of Pompeii. We have the careful work of archaeologists to thank.

VOCABULARY

immense (i MENS) *adj.* huge

On the afternoon of August 24, in the year 79, Vesuvius awoke from its long sleep. The first explosion from the volcano created panic in Pompeii. Many more explosions followed. By the next morning Pompeii was buried under 12 feet of hot ash, rocks, and debris. Few people survived. Anyone who did manage to escape and who returned to Pompeii would have been lost in a strange landscape. They might **question** that Pompeii had ever really been there. Earthquakes caused by the eruption of Vesuvius had created new hills and valleys. The city had vanished. Pompeii's secrets would remain hidden for centuries.

The Rediscovery of a Buried City

For nearly 1600 years, Pompeii lay buried and forgotten. New towns, such as Naples and Torre Annunziata, grew up around the ancient site. In 1592, the citizens of Torre Annunziata came up with a plan. The townspeople wanted to **utilize** water from the nearby Sarno River. They hired Italian architect Domenico Fontana to **undertake** the construction of a tunnel. It would be dug across the plateau where Pompeii had once stood. As Fontana's workmen started cutting through the rock, they began to uncover many statues and wall paintings. Their discoveries, however, did not interest Fontana. He decided not to stop work. He did not want to fully **investigate** what they had found.

In 1734, Spain conquered both Sicily and Naples. Several years later, Spain's King Charles III ordered the

6

King Charles III hoped to find treasures in Pompeii.

first official excavation of Pompeii. His **intent** was to find treasures to enrich the royal court. Charles hired a military engineer named Alcubierre to supervise the work. Alcubierre knew of the underground tunnel that had been dug over a century earlier by Domenico Fontana. He hoped he would be able to follow it to the ruins of ancient Pompeii. Unlike Fontana, Alcubierre wanted to **examine** what was there. He hoped to find objects of value.

VOCABULARY

question (KWES chuhn) *v.* have doubts about something or tell someone about those doubts

utilize (YOO tuh lyz) *v.* put to use; use something for a particular purpose

undertake (un der TAYK) *v.* take upon oneself; agree to do

investigate (in VEST tuh gayt) *v.* try to find out the truth about something, such as a crime, an accident, or a scientific problem

intent (in TENT) *n.* purpose; object; aim

examine (eg ZAM uhn) *v.* look at something carefully in order to make a decision, find something, or check something

7

An Amazing Find!

Twenty days after Alcubierre's crew of 24 men began digging, they made a **significant** find. They uncovered the skeleton of a man who had died during the erup-

This skeleton was unearthed at Pompeii. Gold rings with jewels can be seen on the skeleton's hand.

tion of Vesuvius in 79. Near the skeleton Alcubierre found 18 coins. Could the man have been running away from the eruption, carrying what few valuables he had? Was he killed by the ash and debris? These were interesting questions. Yet, Alcubierre did not want to **pursue** them and find possible answers. He had not come to Pompeii to find answers. He had come to find treasures. Days later, Alcubierre's men found ruined structures. These may have been the remains of a private home or public building in Pompeii. In his report on the day of this discovery, Alcubierre wrote, "Nothing was found."

Alcubierre soon lost interest in Pompeii. Teams of workmen **persisted** in digging at the site. In 1771, they made an amazing discovery. A large house was uncovered. Two skeletons were found in the house. One of them was wearing a gold ring and holding a key. Many gold and silver coins were found near this skeleton. The coins were found wrapped in cloth. Perhaps the coins had been locked up. As Vesuvius erupted, the man may have taken the key to get the coins from their hiding place. Then he ran through the house. But he could not escape the ash and debris. He died with the key still in his hand.

VOCABULARY

significant (sig NIF uh kuhnt) *adj.* important

pursue (puhr SOO) *v.* continue doing an activity or trying to achieve something over a long period of time

persisted (puhr SIST id) *v.* refused to give up

The following year even more skeletons were un-covered at the house. Eighteen adults and two children were found together. They were in an underground room. One of the women had a large amount of jewelry. She was wearing necklaces, bracelets, and rings. She was found with the skeleton of a young boy in her arms. Her remains were very well preserved. The excavators were able to **determine** that she was wearing very beautiful and expensive clothing when she died.

Other skeletons found nearby were not dressed the same way. They wore very simple clothes. Many of them were not wearing shoes. Based on this evidence, the

This painting shows what the market in Pompeii might have looked like before the volcano erupted.

diggers who had discovered the skeletons were able to **identify** the woman as the wife of a wealthy man. The other skeletons were probably the remains of her servants. It is also possible that these people were slaves. The young boy the woman was carrying in her arms might have been her son.

VOCABULARY

determine (dee TER muhn) *v.* decide; figure out
identify (eye DEN tuh fy) *v.* recognize; point out

By the end of the eighteenth century, those in charge of uncovering Pompeii began to use a new **strategy**. They started to leave the buildings they found in plain view. Many objects that were not considered valuable were left inside. Pompeii was slowly becoming what it is today: a museum-city open to visitors. People came from all over the world to see the ruins. They also wanted to see the skeletons that had been uncovered.

Tourists look across a grass courtyard at the ruins of Pompeii.

Unfortunately, a number of these tourists stole bones from the skeletons. They took them home as souvenirs. The ancient site of Pompeii was not well guarded. Soon artwork and other artifacts also began to disappear. In addition, in spite of all that had been uncovered, very few questions about Pompeii had been answered. Who were the people who lived here? When and how was the city destroyed? Before these questions could be answered, new **methods** would have to be put in place to uncover and excavate the rest of the ancient city.

The Search for Information

In 1860, Victor Emmanuel II chose Giuseppe Fiorelli to be the Director of Excavations at Pompeii. Victor Emmanuel was the king of Italy at the time. Fiorelli would **implement** new scientific methods for gathering information about Pompeii. These methods would strongly **affect** the future work of archaeologists, even up to the present day. Fiorelli understood that treasure-hunting excavators had ruined a great deal of historical and scientific information over the years. The search for this information would become the **focus** of his work.

VOCABULARY

strategy (STRAT uh jee) *n.* plan for a specific outcome

methods (METH udz) *n.* ways of doing something

implement (IM pluh muhnt) *v.* begin to make a plan or a process happen

affect (uh FEKT) *v.* do something that produces an effect or change in someone or something

focus (FOH kuhs) *n.* center of interest or attention

Fiorelli started by dividing the city into many small regions. He gave every block and building within each region a number for easy identification. This would help him keep good track of the finds as they were made.

Fiorelli asked his workers to **narrow** their focus as they worked. They were not to **proceed** to another part of Pompeii until the area they were uncovering had been completely examined.

Fiorelli was also responsible for the now-famous plaster casts of Pompeii's victims. Many of the dead were unable to escape the city. They were buried in the thick volcanic ash. Eventually, the ashes hardened and the bodies turned to dust. **Embedded** cavities of human-shaped spaces were found in the thick layer of volcanic material. Fiorelli decided to pour liquid plaster into the cavities. He hoped the plaster would reproduce images of the victims. The technique worked well. Fiorelli's casts revealed facial features. They also showed folds in clothing and even hairstyles. Giuseppe Fiorelli also introduced an entirely

This plaster cast shows one of the victims killed by the eruption of Mount Vesuvius.

This plaster cast shows another victim of the eruption.

new system for the excavation. Fiorelli stopped uncovering the streets first, which had been done to excavate the houses from the ground floor up. Instead, he uncovered the houses from the top down. This was a better way of preserving everything that was discovered. The information that was gathered during the excavations could then be used as a guide. Fiorelli used it to restore both the ancient buildings and their interiors.

VOCABULARY

narrow (NAR oh) *v.* decrease in width, extent, or scope; restrict

proceed (proh SEED) *v.* continue to do something that has already been started

embedded (em BED uhd) *adj.* firmly fixed in surrounding material

Return from the Ashes

This new method of excavation launched a new era in the rediscovery of Pompeii. Fiorelli wasn't looking for treasure. He was looking for information, and he found it. Pompeii's streets were frozen in time. Through his work, Fiorelli was able to carefully **study** what he had found. Soon, he was able to answer many questions about what life had been like in an ancient Roman city. In the marketplace, he found loaves of bread. They were fresh from the oven. Many were still stamped with the baker's name. Studying them revealed what kind of grain the people of Pompeii had used to bake bread. Plates of whole eggs were found in the temple of the goddess Isis. The eggs were ready to be eaten for lunch by priests before the eruption.

The ruins of houses offered a glimpse of what life was like for the wealthy. Fiorelli found lavish homes. They had marble floors and beautiful mosaics on the walls. These are pictures or designs made with small pieces of colored material such as glass or tile stuck onto a surface. The public buildings Fiorelli uncovered showed that the people of Pompeii enjoyed entertainment. They also liked sporting events. They could watch races and wrestling in the gymnasium. They could view plays in the city's theater. Or they could go to the giant amphitheater to watch fights between men and wild animals.

VOCABULARY

study (STUD ee) v. apply your mind to; try to learn or understand by reading or thinking

The homes of the wealthy residents of Pompeii were covered with beautiful mosaics and paintings.

Fiorelli died in January 1896. In the last years of his life, his students Michele Ruggiero, Giulio De Petra, Ettore Pais, and Antonio Sogliano continued Fiorelli's work. They began to restore the roofs of the houses with wood and tiles. This protected the remaining wall paintings and mosaics inside.

Fiorelli's students had learned how to **prioritize** their work according to the importance of what they were finding. They learned this and the method of

studying archaeological sites layer by layer at a training school Fiorelli had founded. Along with the uncovering and restoration of Pompeii, this school was Fiorelli's greatest **achievement**.

VOCABULARY

prioritize (pry OHR uh tyz) *v.* put several jobs or problems in order of importance, so that you can deal with the most important ones first

achievement (uh CHEEV muhnt) *n.* something important that you succeed in doing by your own efforts

These ruins were buried under about 4 meters (13 feet) of hot volcanic ash.

In 1924, archaeologist Amadeo Maiuri began to carry on the work begun by Fiorelli. Under Maiuri, the work at Pompeii became even more thorough. Slowly and carefully, soil and volcanic debris were removed. Maiuri felt it was **essential** to note the position of every piece of plaster and brickwork as it was found. This information was carefully recorded. A photograph was then taken to **reinforce** the written record. If an object needed to be restored, it was carefully removed. Then it was returned to the exact location where it was originally discovered.

Because of the careful excavations of Pompeii, today tourists can see what an ancient Roman city looked like.

Thanks to the careful work of Fiorelli and Maiuri, Pompeii today is an open-air museum. It gives visitors a snapshot of what a Roman city looked like 2,000 years ago. Much of our knowledge of life in the ancient Roman Empire comes from the beautiful houses, paintings, and pottery that were uncovered at Pompeii. Even more important, the pioneering efforts of Fiorelli and Maiuri led to new, more scientific methods for gathering information about the ancient world.

Discussion Questions

1. How do you suppose people could forget that the city of Pompeii had ever existed?

2. What was Giuseppe Fiorelli most interested in finding through his work at Pompeii? How did this drive affect the way he wanted the work done?

3. We can learn much about Pompeii by studying the ruins. However, we cannot learn everything. What kinds of information would you like to know about everyday life in this ancient city? What is missing that might have given us access to that type of knowledge?

VOCABULARY

essential (uh SEN shuhl) *adj.* basic; necessary

reinforce (ree in FOHRS) *v.* give support to an opinion, idea, or feeling, and make it stronger

IDENTIFYING BIRDS

There are some birds that almost anyone can **identify**. Just about everyone knows what a crow looks like. Most people have seen robins and sparrows. Chickadees are pretty common, as are seagulls. But what if you see a bird that you have never seen before? How can you find out what kind it is?

There's nothing birdwatchers like more than seeing a new kind of bird. When they do, they use some simple **methods** to figure out what the bird is. You can use these methods, too. You can learn how to gather the information that will help you **pursue** your aim: to identify birds.

A Winged Mystery

Startling Sighting In February of 2004, a man named Gene Sparling was kayaking in the Cache River National Wilderness of Arkansas. The area he was in was a bayou. It was swampy, with many old trees. He saw a very large bird. It flew toward him and landed on a nearby tree. He watched it with the **intent** of identifying it. It was large and moved with a jerky motion. It looked to him like an ivory-billed woodpecker. This is a bird that has not been seen since 1944. Everyone thought it was extinct—that there were none left on Earth.

   Shortly afterward, a birdwatcher captured the woodpecker on videotape. However, the quality of the tape was bad. Experts were not convinced. Ornithologists, scientists who study birds, looked at the tape. One said that the wings of the bird in the video had the wrong colors to be an ivory-billed woodpecker. He claimed it was a pileated woodpecker, a much more common bird. This bird is very similar in shape, size, and color to an ivory-billed woodpecker. Another ornithologist insisted that the bird in the video flew too quickly to be a pileated woodpecker.

VOCABULARY

identify (eye DEN tuh fy) *v.* recognize; point out

methods (METH udz) *n.* ways of doing something

pursue (puhr SOO) *v.* continue doing an activity or trying to achieve something over a long period of time

intent (in TENT) *n.* purpose; object; aim

Douglas Zollner, from the Nature Conservancy, looks for signs of the rediscovered ivory-billed woodpecker. Jeremy Whiley, of the U.S. Fish and Wildlife Service, looks on.

Experts Join In Ornithologists came to the area to **participate** in a search. Several of them saw the bird, too. They described it. It had white wing edges. There was a narrow red crest on its head. A white line ran from its wings up its neck. One scientist heard the bird double-knocking on a tree trunk. He said this was a sound no other bird could **imitate**. It had to be an ivory-billed woodpecker.

Other ornithologists still did not think the bird was an ivory-billed woodpecker. They said it must be a pile-ated woodpecker. How could they **determine** which kind of bird it was?

There are six main ways that birdwatchers **distinguish** one bird from another. Their methods **utilize** the senses—sight and hearing—and they compare unknown birds to known birds. You can use these methods to identify birds, too. In fact, you can use them to decide for yourself if the mystery bird was a pileated woodpecker or an ivory-billed woodpecker!

Identifying by Habitat

When you **undertake** the task of identifying a bird, you can start with its habitat. A bird's habitat is the area where it lives. Each habitat has its own climate, plants, and landforms. Each species of bird likes some habitats and doesn't like others. The habitat where a bird lives depends on many things, including what the bird eats and where it nests. Different foods are available in each habitat. Different places to nest are found in each area.

VOCABULARY

participate (pahr TIS uh payt) *v.* take part in an activity or event

imitate (IM i tayt) *v.* copy; mimic

determine (dee TER muhn) *v.* decide; figure out

distinguish (di STING wish) *v.* recognize or understand the difference between two similar things or people

utilize (YOO tuh lyz) *v.* put to use; use something for a particular purpose

undertake (un der TAYK) *v.* take upon oneself; agree to do

25

There are many different habitats. Listed here are the most common habitats in the United States. Also listed are a common bird and a rare or endangered bird found in each habitat.

- Salt water (including open water, rocky shores, and beaches). A common bird found here is the herring gull. An endangered bird is the black-footed albatross.
- Fresh water (including lakes, rivers, streams, and marshes). A common bird found in fresh water is the wood duck. An endangered one is the whooping crane.
- Forests (including pine and coniferous forests and deciduous forests). A common bird in this habitat is the blue jay. An endangered one is the cerulean warbler.
- Grasslands (including prairies, plains, and meadows). A common bird found here is the Western meadowlark. An endangered bird is the greater prairie chicken.
- Deserts (including mesas, scrubland, and bare mountains). A common desert bird is the lesser prairie chicken. An endangered one is the Gunnison sage grouse.
- Tundra (cold northern areas). A common tundra bird is the snow bunting. An endangered bird is the bristle-thighed curlew.
- Urban and suburban areas. Chimney swifts are commonly found here. An endangered bird is the green parakeet.

Each of these habitats is home to many different bird species. Some species overlap habitats. Most birds that are found in urban and suburban areas also live in other areas. When you know a bird's habitat, you have already learned a lot about it.

The pileated woodpecker usually lives in a forest habitat. It can also be found in suburban areas with tall trees.

The ivory-billed woodpecker was found in mature cypress or southern pine forests. It usually **resided** in swampy areas.

At one time, ivory-billed woodpeckers could be found in South Carolina swamps like this.

VOCABULARY

reside (ree ZYD) *v.* live in a particular place

Identifying by Size

The next step in identifying a bird is to check its size. Birdwatchers do this by comparing the size of an unknown bird to the size of a known bird. They often break down sizes into seven categories.

- Very small (hummingbirds and goldfinches)
- Sparrow-sized (warblers and house sparrows)
- Robin-sized (American robins and mourning doves)
- Pigeon-sized (rock doves and sharp-shinned hawks)
- Crow-sized (wood ducks and laughing gulls)
- Goose-sized (white ibises and anhingas)
- Very large (bald eagles and brown pelicans)

The size of the bird does not include the length of its neck, legs, or tail. It just refers to the size of its body.

The length of the adult pileated woodpecker is 16–19 inches (crow-sized).

The length of the adult ivory-billed woodpecker is 20 inches (crow-sized).

Identifying by Shape and Posture

In Good Shape Looking closely at a bird's shape can ==enable== a birdwatcher to identify the bird. Some birds are stocky. They have plump bodies and look round. Other birds are slender. Their bodies are thin.

The shapes of a bird's head, bill, tail, and wings are also ==significant==. These shapes can tell you a lot about the bird. A water bird with a long, straight bill probably uses it to poke the sand or mud for food. A bird with a short, heavy bill can use it to crack open seeds. A bird with wide, rounded wings probably soars in flight.

VOCABULARY

enable (en AY buhl) *v.* give someone what they need to be able to do something

significant (sig NIF uh kuhnt) *adj.* important

Ruffed grouse like this one are common in aspen forests with dense undergrowth. It feeds on the buds of aspen trees.

Stand by Me A bird's posture can provide a **key** method of identification. Some birds are horizontal. They have short legs and slender bodies. They usually feed while flying. Other birds are vertical. They sit upright to look for prey.

The great blue heron stands about 4 feet tall and has a wingspan of 7 feet. It can be found in many wetland environments.

Pileated woodpeckers are stocky. They have a pointed crest on their heads. They are vertical in posture.	Ivory-billed woodpeckers are stocky. They have a pointed crest and are vertical in posture.

Identifying by Color and Pattern

Every Color in the World Birdwatchers study a bird's color to try to identify it. First, they figure out the main color of the bird. This is likely to be blue, black, white, red, orange, yellow, brown, olive, or gray. There are **diverse** shades of each of these colors. Some birds' colors are shiny. Some feathers shimmer. Some are dull.

Few birds have only a single color. One example is the crow, which is entirely black. The painted bunting, on the other hand, is blue, green, red, and purple. A bird's coloring is a strong clue to its identity.

Looking at Patterns Once you know a bird's colors, you can **proceed** to look at its field marks, or patterns. The most important field marks can be found on a bird's head or wings. Stripes, rings, and patches can make a bird distinctive. They may be spotted or streaked. They may have colored crowns or eyebrows. Their beaks, breasts, wings, or tails may be colored and patterned.

VOCABULARY

key (KEE) *adj.* important
diverse (duh VERS) *adj.* various; with different characteristics
proceed (proh SEED) *v.* continue to do something that has already been started

A pileated woodpecker has wings with trailing dark edges. When it is perched, a small white wing patch can be seen. A white line runs from the bill down the neck into the side. The bill is black, shading to yellow. The crest is red and reaches the forehead in the male. It is shorter in the female.

An ivory-billed woodpecker has white trailing wing edges. A large white wing patch can be seen when it is at rest. A white line runs from below the eye down the neck and onto the back. The bill is large and ivory-colored. The male has a curved, painted red crest with a black forehead. The female's crest is black.

Identifying by Behavior

Actions Speak Loudly The way a bird acts is its behavior. Each species has different behaviors. These include the way they eat and what they eat; how they swim, dive, and move; and the way they fly. For example, some water birds swim on the surface. Some swim lower in the water. Some, like the anhinga, swim with only their head out of the water. Many ducks "tip up," tilting their bodies so their tails point up. They do this to reach the plants at the bottom.

Some birds, such as the bald eagle, dive from the air into the water for fish. Some, such as the cormorant, pump their wings for the **purpose** of drying them. Some owls tilt their heads. Nuthatches climb down tree trunks upside-down. Roadrunners run quickly. American redstarts fan out their tails. American crows will chase other birds that threaten their nests. Gulls will steal food from each other.

Flying By Flying behaviors also differ. Bald eagles soar. Loons fly in a straight line. Sandhill cranes fly with their necks stretched out. Hummingbirds hover. Wild turkeys

VOCABULARY

purpose (PER puhs) *n.* intention; plan

beat their wings quickly. Great egrets beat their wings slowly. Blackbirds fly in large groups, and Canada geese fly in a V formation.

Observe a bird's behavior. What does it eat? How does it move? How does it fly? All these characteristics will give important clues to its identity.

The pileated woodpecker drums on trees slowly and loudly for two to three seconds at a time. Its flight is slow and sweeping.

The ivory-billed woodpecker gives a loud double-rap drum on trees. Its flight is swift and straight.

Many Canada geese fly south in winter and fly north in summer. Large groups fly in a V formation.

This clay-colored sparrow in Montana has an unusual song. It makes a series of two to five slow, low-pitched buzzes.

Identifying by Voice

The final method of identification is by voice. Bird noises are identified as either calls or songs. Calls are short, often one syllable. They are used to show fear or alarm, to contact or **respond** to other birds, or to threaten predators. They can be heard at any time of year. Songs are longer. They are used to claim territory or to interest a mate. Bird songs are usually heard in spring and summer.

The sounds of calls and songs are often described as lisping, trilling, buzzing, cooing, whistling, and warbling. The calls or songs of many birds actually **evoke** their names. Among these are bobwhite, chickadee, phoebe, catbird, and whippoorwill.

A pileated woodpecker's call sounds like *kuk kuk*. It may also make a call that sounds like *yucka yucka yucka*.

An ivory-billed woodpecker's call sounds like *yank yank yank*.

Be a Birdwatcher

With a pair of binoculars, a field guide to birds, and your own senses, you can probably identify almost any bird you see. The methods you've read about will help you. Notice a bird's habitat, size, shape, posture, color, and markings. Observe its behavior and flight. Listen to its voice. Each of these details will **contribute** to your identification. Even just a quick glimpse of a bird can give you enough information to **hypothesize** about its identity. If the bird will **cooperate** by staying in sight long enough, you can be even more certain of your identification. Watching and identifying birds can **enrich** your understanding of nature and the world around you.

VOCABULARY

respond (ri SPAHND) *v.* react to something that has been said or done

evoke (ee VOHK) *v.* produce a strong feeling or memory in someone

contribute (kuhn TRIB yoot) *v.* give money, help, or ideas to something that other people are also involved in

hypothesize (hy PAHTH uh syz) *n.* propose an unproven theory to explain certain facts

cooperate (koh AHP uhr ayt) *v.* act or work together with another or others for a common purpose

enrich (en RICH) *v.* improve the quality of something, especially by adding things to it

Look closely at the differences between the ivory-billed woodpecker on the left and the pileated woodpecker on the right.

Can You Solve It?

Now you can put what you've learned to the test. You've read about the woodpecker sightings in Arkansas. You know the characteristics of the pileated woodpecker and the ivory-billed woodpecker. **Study** the pictures of the two kinds of woodpeckers. Look at the descriptions of habitat, size, shape, posture, coloring, markings, behavior, and voice. Compare them to the description of the bird in Arkansas. What do you think? Has the ivory-billed woodpecker been rediscovered?

Discussion Questions

1. Which method do you think is most important for making an identification of an unknown bird?

2. Why is it important to find out if the Arkansas mystery bird is really an ivory-billed woodpecker or not?

3. Do you think the mystery bird is an ivory-billed woodpecker? Why or why not? What information did you use to make your decision?

VOCABULARY

study (STUD ee) *v.* apply your mind to; try to learn or understand by reading or thinking

The Story of
American Sign Language

Language is a way of gathering information that people throughout the world share. American Sign Language is a special language. It enables deaf and hard-of-hearing people to communicate. Perhaps you have seen people using sign language. It is made up of hand signs, as well as other gestures and facial expressions. This form of communication is a complete language. It is rich with descriptions and feelings. In the silent world of the deaf, as in the hearing world, the need to communicate ideas and to gather information is extremely important. American Sign Language fulfills this **essential** need. How did this language develop? What makes it a language apart from the English used by hearing people? Can we all benefit from its use? Let's find out.

These deaf boys communicate using sign language.

What Is American Sign Language?

American Sign Language (known as *ASL,* for short) is a language for the deaf. It is a complete language, apart from the English that hearing people use when they speak. ASL uses signs made by the hands along with facial expressions, postures of the body, mouth movements, and other gestures.

VOCABULARY

essential (uh SEN shuhl) *adj.* basic; necessary

Young deaf actors rehearse for their performance of a play.

This special language is a first language for many deaf people in the United States and Canada. This means it is their native, or first-learned, language, much the way English is the first language of most hearing North Americans. ASL is a second language for many others. It is taught in schools to **enable** hearing people to use it. ASL is thought to be the fourth most commonly spoken language in North America. Over 500,000 people use it.

Does it surprise you to know that American Sign Language is a rich and expressive language even though

it does not use spoken words? This is done by the use of many hand signs and other gestures. It's possible to think of ASL as a "three-dimensional" language that uses the space around the speaker as part of its vocabulary. For hearing people, sounds are heard during a conversation. In contrast, the **strategy** of deaf people is to use their eyes to see a conversation.

Vocabulary

enable (en AY buhl) *v.* give someone what they need to be able to do something

strategy (STRAT uh jee) *n.* plan for a specific outcome

Although North Americans and the British both speak English, ASL does not share many signs with British Sign Language. This is because ASL did not develop out of the sign language used in England. This means that deaf people from America and England cannot easily understand each other's sign language. In fact, there are many different sign languages throughout the world.

The deaf **community** did **establish** a limited number of international signs. This enables signers from different countries to communicate at international events. In general, however, the sign languages used in various countries are not interchangeable.

What Is the History of ASL and Other Sign Languages?

Early Sign Languages American Sign Language was not the first sign language in the world. The deaf of other countries had already created their own forms of sign language long ago.

Throughout history, hearing people have also used sign language. For example, groups of Native Americans spoke many different languages. To understand each other, they used hand signs. Monks in Europe who had taken a vow of silence also developed hand signals to **maintain** communication.

Even today, hearing people use many gestures and facial expressions to share thoughts or feelings. These things are understood without a word being uttered. For example, a thumbs-up sign means things are going well. If you see someone holding his or her nose, however, chances are something smells bad!

A Native American teaches sign language to a tourist
in the Black Hills of South Dakota.

Martha's Vineyard Sign Language On Martha's
Vineyard, an island off the coast of Massachusetts, an
interesting thing happened. The families who settled
there carried a gene that caused deafness. Eventually,
during the eighteenth century, almost every family on
the island had at least one deaf member.

A form of sign language emerged that was used and
understood by everyone living on the island. Because
it was used so much, this sign language was quickly
learned by all the youngsters. Both deaf and hearing

VOCABULARY

community (kuh MYOO nuh tee) *n.* group of people living
together; people united by a common problem or interest
establish (uh STAB lish) *v.* make sure of; determine; set up
maintain (MAYN tayn) *v.* make something continue in the same
way or at the same standard as before

children learned it at an early age when language is most easily picked up. This was a **significant** development. It showed how a community of deaf and hearing people could adapt to the situation and **benefit** from sign language.

The Growth of American Sign Language

The American Sign Language used today grew out of a combination of native, or folk, signs used in America among deaf people and French Sign Language (FSL). The work of Thomas Hopkins Gallaudet was essential to this process.

In the early 1800s, this young teacher was asked by a neighbor if he would work with the man's deaf daughter. Her name was Alice Cogswell. At the time, there was a **bias** against deaf people. Many unfairly felt that the deaf could not be educated. Gallaudet strongly disagreed. He decided to try to help young Alice. He traveled to England in order to learn the **methods** used there to communicate with the deaf.

This statue shows Thomas Gallaudet with one of the children his school benefited.

Unfortunately, Gallaudet could not **resolve** his differences with the school for the deaf there. The family who taught in the school wanted to place many restrictions upon the way their methods would be used in America. Gallaudet did not feel this was in the best interest of the deaf children he wanted to teach.

While in England, however, Gallaudet met two Frenchmen. They were Abbe Sicard and Laurent Clerc. Sicard was the director of the French Institute for the Deaf in Paris. Clerc was a deaf instructor at the school. Gallaudet explained his mission. The Frenchmen encouraged him to return to Paris with them. They wanted to **cooperate** with Gallaudet and to teach him French Sign Language.

Gallaudet was making fast progress in his studies, but ran out of money to stay in France. He asked Clerc to return to the United States in order to help him start a school for the deaf. On the journey to America, Gallaudet taught Clerc English. The Frenchman continued to teach sign language to Gallaudet.

VOCABULARY

significant (sig NIF uh kuhnt) *adj.* important

benefit (BEN uh fit) *v.* bring advantages to someone or improve their lives in some way

bias (BY uhs) *n.* an opinion about whether a person, group, or idea is good or bad, that influences how you deal with it

methods (METH udz) *n.* ways of doing something

resolve (ri ZAHLV) *v.* find a satisfactory way of dealing with a problem or difficulty; settle

cooperate (koh AHP uhr ayt) *v.* act or work together with another or others for a common purpose

When they arrived in Hartford, Connecticut, in 1817, the two men began the American School for the Deaf. The school was a groundbreaking **achievement** at that time. It would **affect** the way society regarded the deaf. Now Alice Cogswell and others like her would be able to get an education. The school still exists today. It continues to **enrich** the lives of the deaf, their families, and our society.

Together Gallaudet and Clerc worked with deaf American children to teach them a new language called American Sign Language. The men decided to **integrate** the signs used in FSL along with the signs and gestures already in use among deaf Americans. They also added new signs and movements to create ASL. FSL and ASL are not the same language. They do, however, share a great deal of the same vocabulary because of the **influence** of FSL upon ASL.

What Makes ASL a Language?

People who study languages have found that each language has certain basic characteristics. American Sign Language is no exception. It is not an adaptation of English with mimed gestures. Instead it is a separate language. It has its own rules for grammar, the order of words in a sentence, and punctuation.

Linguists, the people who study languages, have broken down the signs of ASL into three groups. They **identify** one group as *transparent signs*. These are signs for which nonsigners can guess the meaning. The second group is made up of *translucent signs*. These are signs

Teacher Debi Schaefer signs the word *dad* to Collin Sauber and his young sister in a sign language class.

that make sense to nonsigners after they are explained. The third group has *opaque signs.* This means that non-signers cannot guess what these signs mean.

VOCABULARY

achievement (uh CHEEV muhnt) *n.* something important that you succeed in doing by your own efforts

affect (uh FEKT) *v.* do something that produces an effect or change in someone or something

enrich (en RICH) *v.* improve the quality of something, especially by adding things to it

integrate (IN tuh grayt) *v.* remove all barriers and allow access to all

influence (IN floo uhns) *n.* power to affect others

identify (eye DEN tuh fy) *v.* recognize; point out

49

Researchers did experiments in which all three kinds of signs were used in conversation. They found that nonsigners could not understand a conversation of continuous sign language. These linguists **contend** that this proves that ASL is a distinct language.

Punctuation is different in ASL, too. For example, there is no sign for a question mark. Instead, a question is shown by facial expression, such as raising one's eyebrows and widening the eyes.

Verb tense is also different in ASL. All sentences are signed in the present tense. Then, a "comment" sign is added to show whether the event described already happened or will happen in the future. The order of words in a sentence in ASL is often different, as well. For example, in English, one might say: *Roll the red ball now.* In ASL, the order of words is: *Now ball red roll*.

When more than one person is being described in a conversation in ASL, the first time a person is mentioned, he or she is described. Then the person being talked about is assigned a space around the speaker. After that, the speaker points to that space to refer to the person. There may be as many as eight different "people locations" in an ASL conversation.

Fingerspelling and Counting

There are signs that correspond to each letter of the alphabet. They are used to *fingerspell* the names of people,

VOCABULARY

contend (kuhn TEND) *v.* compete against someone in order to gain something; claim to be a fact

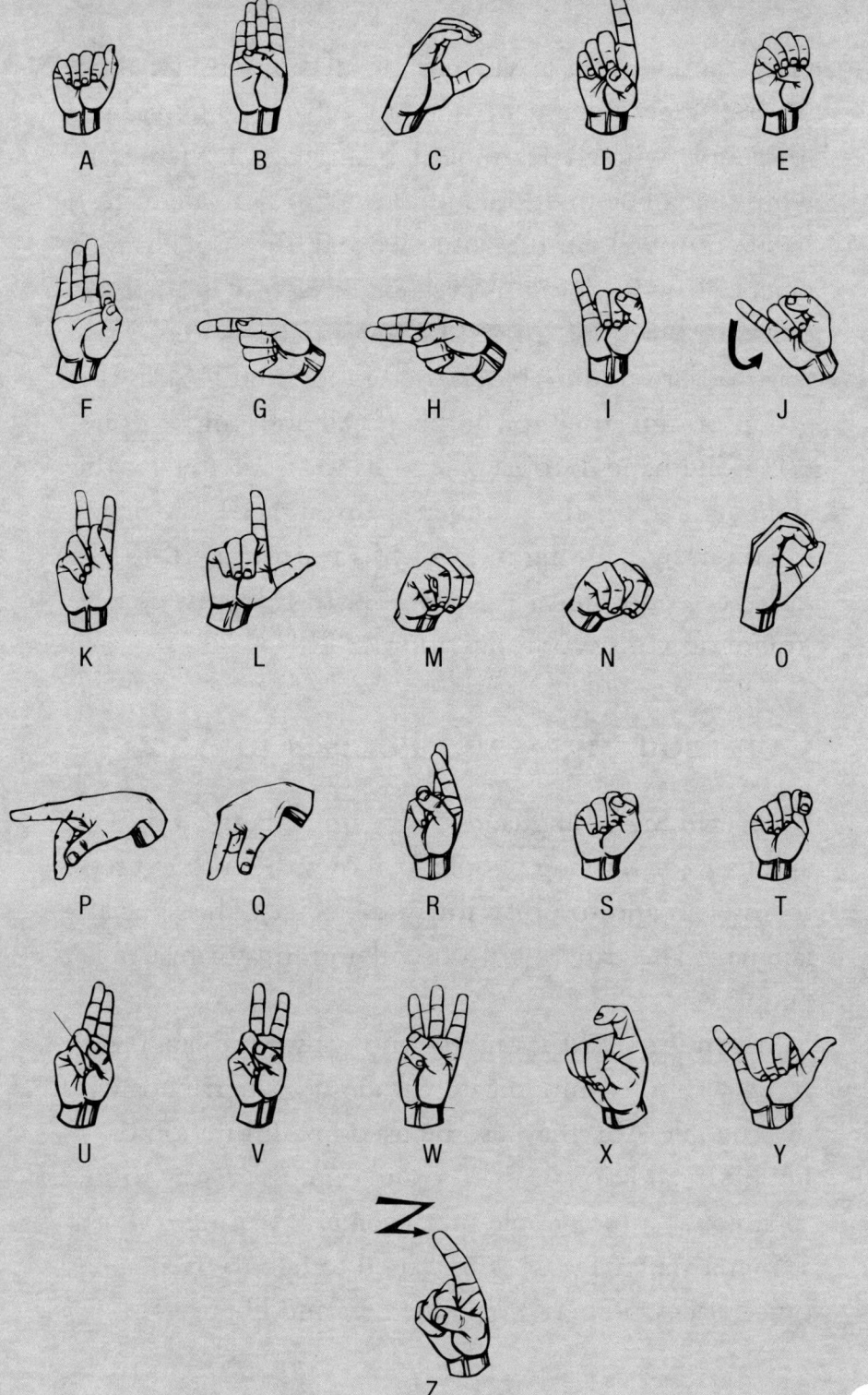

places, and words for which there are no signs. The signs used in fingerspelling are one of the basic building blocks for people who are learning sign language. If there is a word that a beginner does not know in sign language, he or she can spell out the entire word. This is not always a practical way to speak, as it takes a long time to spell out every word with its corresponding English letters.

Another building block used in learning ASL is the group of signs used for numbers. All counting is done using one hand. Look at the signs for the letters of the alphabet and for the numbers 1 through 10. Try practicing them by standing in front of a mirror. Imitate each sign. Try counting to 10. Then fingerspell your name. You're on your way to learning ASL!

Common Signs and Phrases in ASL

American Sign Language is very important for deaf and hard-of-hearing people. It allows them to express themselves and to contribute to society. This special language also can be both useful and fun for hearing people.

If you learn ASL, you will know a second language. It is a way to communicate with and make friends with deaf people. ASL may also be used in a future job or hobby. In addition, it is a fun and expressive way to speak to anyone. Some people may even enjoy using ASL as a "secret" language. It can be used to talk to friends in quiet places, such as movie theaters and libraries.

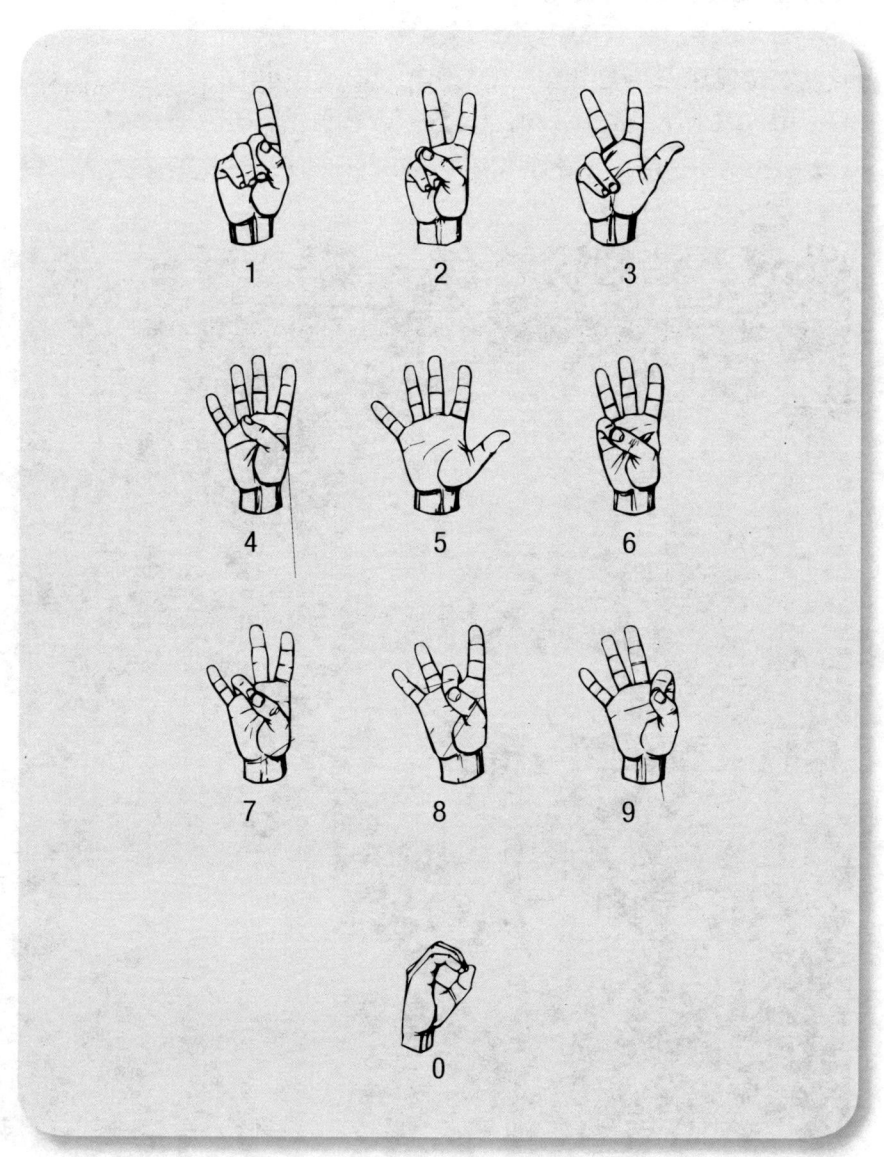

VOCABULARY

imitate (IM i tayt) *v.* copy; mimic

contribute (kuhn TRIB yoot) *v.* give money, help, or ideas to something that other people are also involved in

Current Trends

Baby Sign Language A popular, simpler form of ASL is called Baby Sign Language. Many parents and researchers believe infants as young as six or seven months

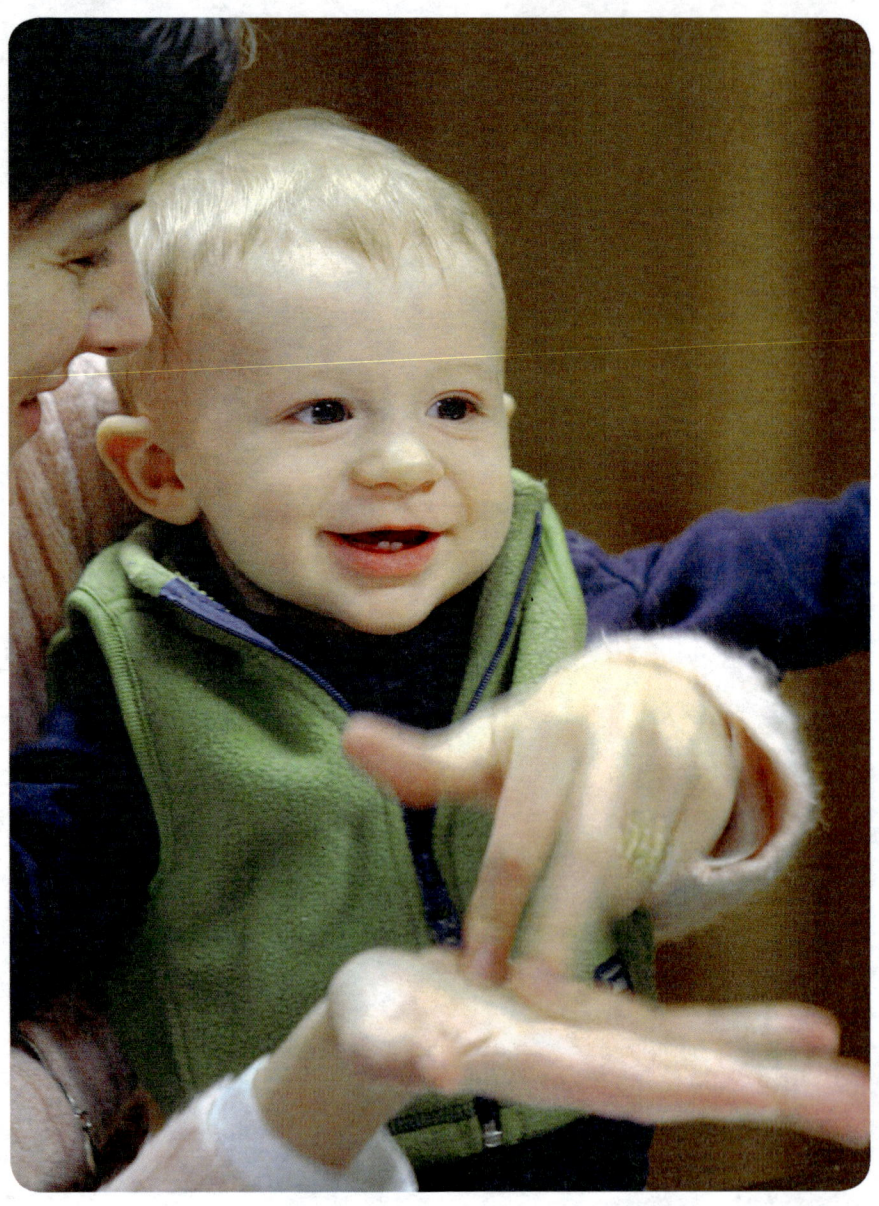

old can begin to learn how to sign. First, parents learn to use simple signs for such words as *more* or *milk* with their child. When the baby or toddler uses the sign, the parent responds.

This popular method is said to reduce the frustration that toddlers **confront** when they try to communicate before they have mastered spoken language. Baby Signing is recommended by some. Others believe more study is needed to be sure it does not interfere with learning spoken English.

Expression Through the Arts At the Lexington School for the Deaf in Queens, New York, students are encouraged to use ASL to write and perform plays about their experiences. An interpreter stands near the stage and signs the action of the play for the audience.

During the performance of one play, the deaf youngsters dance to hip-hop and rap music. This music, with its heavy beat, causes vibrations in the air and on the floor, which the deaf dancers can feel. This lets them "hear" the music and dance to it. This new **direction** in education is a valuable opportunity for deaf students to express themselves.

VOCABULARY

confront (kuhn FRONT) *v.* deal with something very difficult or bad in a brave and determined way; accuse someone of doing something by showing them proof

direction (duh REK shuhn) *n.* general purpose or aim; the general way in which someone or something changes or develops

Gallaudet University This school, named after Thomas Hopkins Gallaudet, provides a college education for deaf and hard-of-hearing students. Located in Washington, D.C., Gallaudet has more than 1,500 students.

Classes provide students with a high-quality education that allows them to learn and to become productive citizens. The school offers many kinds of career development programs for the deaf. Gallaudet is also a leader in research on the language, culture, and history of the deaf.

Graduating seniors at Gallaudet University sign the national anthem at the graduation ceremony.

Language Holds the Key!

American Sign Language, like other languages, is a way for people to gather and to share information. The development of ASL is an amazing story of how individuals, despite difficult challenges, will always find ways to **prevail** in their need to communicate.

Discussion Questions

1. Each of our five senses helps us gather information. Name each of the senses and give examples of the kinds of information each sense provides. Tell why each kind of information is important.

2. Scientists believe that deafness is more isolating for a person than blindness is. Why do you think this is so?

3. Do you think schools should offer American Sign Language as a choice for learning a second language much the way French or Spanish are offered? Why or why not?

4. Imagine being a deaf person in the days before schools for the deaf were established. What messages would you most have wanted to communicate to those in the hearing world around you?

VOCABULARY

prevail (pree VAYL) *v.* gain the advantage or mastery; be victorious; triumph

The Measure of a Good Cook

Long ago, cooking **methods** and recipes were only taught person to person. Nothing was written down. Very little information about cooking was precise. As you watched soup being made, the cook might say, "Add about this much chicken stock." If you weren't standing there, you would have no idea what that meant! Later, you might not remember how much chicken stock the cook had actually added. If you had no experience with making soup, you might give up before you even got started. What can help to make cooking less stressful? Let's read and find out.

The Early Days of Cookbooks

As early as 1639, the first "cookery books" were found in England. These cooking guides were written for chefs to use.

By the mid 1700s, the guides finally focused on common household cooking. In 1796, the first American cookbook was published.

These early cookbooks listed the ingredients to use. They described what to do with them. Information about how to **measure** those ingredients varied widely, however. There was no universal set of measurements. Instead, the measurements were **diverse** and descriptive. They might say, "Take a lump of butter the size of a duck's egg." Or, "Add a grapefruit spoon full of salt."

VOCABULARY

methods (METH udz) *n.* ways of doing something

measure (MEZH uhr) *v.* find the size, length, or amount of something using standard units

diverse (duh VERS) *adj.* various; with different characteristics

It was an American, Fannie Merritt Farmer, who made cooking more scientific. Her famous *Boston Cooking-School Cook Book* was published in 1896. At the top of each recipe, she listed the ingredients with precise measurements to use. Words such as *measuring cup* and *level tablespoon* appeared for the first time. Her **intent** was to make it possible for even new cooks to follow a recipe.

Farmer's style was to list ingredients in the order they are used. She then gave step-by-step directions. This would **prevail** as the best style of recipe. Open any cookbook today, and this is still what you will see.

This 1950s photo shows a young woman studying a recipe in the *Boston Cooking-School Cook Book*.

Systems of Measurement

The measuring system that **evolved** in the United States is based on volume. It uses teaspoons, tablespoons, cups, pints, and so on. The chart below can help you **determine** how measurements relate to one another.

3 teaspoons = 1 tablespoon	1 tablespoon = $1/2$ fluid ounce
4 tablespoons = $1/4$ cup	1 cup = 8 fluid ounces
8 tablespoons = $1/2$ cup	2 cups = 1 pint
16 tablespoons = 1 cup	4 cups = 1 quart
	4 quarts = 1 gallon

VOCABULARY

intent (in TENT) *n.* purpose; object; aim

prevail (pree VAYL) *v.* gain the advantage or mastery; be victorious; triumph

evolved (ee VAHLVD) *v.* grew gradually; developed

determine (dee TER muhn) *v.* decide; figure out

All major countries in the world except the United States use the metric system of measurement. It was first developed in 1790. It was meant to **establish** a very simple set of universal measurements.

The metric system is easy to learn. It is based on multiples of ten. Another **sensible** feature of this system is that volume, weight, and length each have just one basic unit of measurement. Then smaller and larger units are named by adding a prefix. Just think! You would not have to remember teaspoons, tablespoons, cups, pints, quarts, gallons, ounces, pounds. You would just have to know liters and grams.

This French chef uses metric measurements in his recipes.

The chart below lists the metric units and how they match up to the American system. If you ever use a recipe from another country, this will be **key** information to know.

The Metric System and Its Equivalencies	
Volume	
The basic unit of measurement for volume is the **liter.** 1 liter = 1.06 quarts	Smaller amounts are measured in **milliliters.** 5 milliliters = 1 teaspoon A dash of pepper is about 1 milliliter.
Weight	
The basic unit of measurement for weight is the **gram.** 1 gram = 0.035 ounces	Larger amounts are measured in **kilograms.** 1 kilogram = 2.2 pounds 1/8 cup of shredded coconut weighs about 10 grams.
Length	
The basic unit of measurement for length is the **meter.** 1 meter = 1.1 yard	Smaller lengths are measured in **centimeters.** 1 centimeter = 0.4 inch Most cookie sheets are 14 inches long, which is about 35 centimeters.

VOCABULARY

establish (uh STAB lish) *v.* make sure of; determine; set up

sensible (SEN suh buhl) *adj.* wise; intelligent

key (KEE) *adj.* important

Two Kinds Are Better Than One

Ingredients that are measured by volume fall into two categories. Dry ingredients include flour, sugar, salt, baking powder, and baking soda. Wet ingredients include water, milk, cream, and oil. As a result, there are three kinds of measuring devices. These are dry cups, wet cups, and spoons. Dry and wet cups are used for the types of ingredients they name. You can **utilize** spoons for smaller amounts of both types of ingredients.

This picture shows how to level off the flour in a dry measuring cup.

The Things You Need for Cooking

A well-stocked kitchen doesn't only have food. It also includes the things for measuring and preparing food that cooks need. You now know that you need three types of measuring tools.

Dry measuring cups are usually made of plastic or metal. They come in various sizes. You often buy them in sets of 1 cup, $1/2$ cup, $1/3$ cup, $1/4$ cup, and $1/8$ cup. To measure these amounts, fill the cup to the brim. Then use the flat side of a knife to level off the ingredient from rim to rim.

<small>Vocabulary</small>

utilize (YOO tuh lyz) *v.* put to use; use something for a particular purpose

Measuring spoons, wet measuring cups, and a variety of pots and pans are also needed for a well-stocked kitchen.

Wet measuring cups come in different sizes, with 1 cup, 2 cups, and 4 cups being the most common. Cups made of clear glass are best. With these you can easily see the amount of liquid you are measuring. When you use these cups, you must look at the measuring marks at eye level. Set the cup on a level surface. Pour in the liquid. Then crouch down to see if the amount you have poured is at the correct mark.

Measuring spoons are sold in sets. They are usually held together by a ring through the handles. Each set consists of spoons of different sizes—1 tablespoon, 1 teaspoon, 1/2 teaspoon, 1/4 teaspoon, and 1/8 teaspoon. Most of the time, the sizes are stamped on the spoons.

Many recipes also say the types and sizes of pots and pans to use. A well-stocked kitchen includes a variety of sizes and shapes of baking dishes and pans. These items are usually measured in inches. You might use a 9" x 12" pan or a 10" skillet, for example.

Other cookware such as casserole dishes, saucepans, and kettles are specified by the amount they will hold. The recipe might suggest a 3–quart casserole or a 6–quart stock pot, for example.

The sizes of all of these items are usually stamped on them. If you cannot see a label anywhere, measure for yourself! Over time, your cooking experience will **enable** you to know the size of an item just by looking at it.

VOCABULARY

enable (en AY buhl) *v.* give someone what they need to be able to do something

Is "Close Enough" Good Enough?

So, once you have the right measuring devices, how precise do measurements have to be? After all, cooks often change things to suit their own tastes. Suppose a recipe says "1/2 teaspoon of salt." If you really like salt, you can add more. If you don't like salt, you might leave it out altogether. If a recipe you were working from said, "a grapefruit spoon full of salt," it wouldn't matter if you knew what a grapefruit spoon looked like or not. You know how big spoons are in general. Just add the amount of salt you feel would best **enrich** the recipe.

The amount of herbs you add to pasta can vary with your taste, but baking ingredients must be carefully measured.

There are other times, though, when precision is **essential**. For example, if you don't add enough chicken stock to soup, you will end up with a pot full of mushy vegetables. And in baking, you really must get the ingredients right. All kinds of chemical reactions go on inside the oven when you bake. Leave one thing out and your biscuits will be hard and flat instead of light and fluffy! As a beginning baker, you should think of a recipe as more than a **reference**. It should truly be your guide.

VOCABULARY

enrich (en RICH) *v.* improve the quality of something, especially by adding things to it

essential (uh SEN shuhl) *adj.* basic; necessary

reference (REF uhr uhns) *n.* the act of looking at something for information; the book or magazine that you get the information from

Putting It All Together to Cook

You now have good information about measurement and cooking utensils. You have been given some tips that will **benefit** you as a beginning cook. You have a well-stocked kitchen and some great recipes. It's time to **pursue** the art and science of cooking by making a meal!

Should you expect to feel confused at times? Yes! But follow one beginner as he makes a birthday dinner for

A cook's first baking experience can be successful as long as he makes good decisions.

his mom. You might get some great ideas about how to **resolve** cooking problems. Let's follow Zach through his first cooking experience.

Zach begins by choosing recipes for the foods he wants to make. His planned menu includes beef stew, a spinach salad, breadsticks, and a birthday cake. Working from the recipes, Zach makes a detailed list of all the ingredients he needs to buy. At least, Zach thinks it's detailed. When he gets to the store, however, Zach has some moments of confusion. They nearly **evoke** panic in him.

Why, for example, are there so many kinds of flour to choose from? After taking a deep breath, Zach chooses "all-purpose flour." What a good choice!

Zach also worries his way through the fresh vegetable department. His list says that he needs 1 cup of mushrooms and 6 cups of spinach. But both items are sold by ounces, not cups. Zach closes his eyes and pictures the dry cup measurer. He chooses a wrapped container of mushrooms that looks about the same size. He also knows to select one of the bigger bags of spinach. Way to go, Zach!

VOCABULARY

benefit (BEN uh fit) *v.* bring advantages to someone or improve their lives in some way

pursue (puhr SOO) *v.* continue doing an activity or trying to achieve something over a long period of time

resolve (ri ZAHLV) *v.* find a satisfactory way of dealing with a problem or difficulty; settle

evoke (ee VOHK) *v.* produce a strong feeling or memory in someone

Back at home, Zach gets down to cooking. His first questions here also have to do with vegetables. For the stew, he has to chop the various vegetables. The amounts are listed in cups on the recipe. But Zach has no idea how much chopped celery will make up 1½ cups! He decides to chop one stalk at a time, continuing to measure until he has the right amount. This works well. Zach should also remember that cookbooks can be a good **source** of information beyond recipes. Many include sections at the front or back to help new cooks. For example, Zach might have found a chart like the one below if he had looked.

Vegetable Amounts	
If you buy a bunch of 6 to 8 carrots, that is about a pound.	This will give you about 2½ cups of chopped carrots.
You usually buy celery by the bunch.	A medium bunch will give you about 4½ cups of chopped celery.
Peppers are usually sold individually.	A large chopped green pepper yields about 1 cup.
Onions are usually sold by the pound.	One medium chopped onion yields about ½ cup.
Potatoes are sold by the pound.	A cubed potato will give you about ⅔ cup.

Zach has the stew simmering. The dough for the breadsticks is rising. The salad is ready. Now Zach starts on the cake. He needs six tablespoons of butter. How can he go from four sticks of hard butter, making up a pound, to

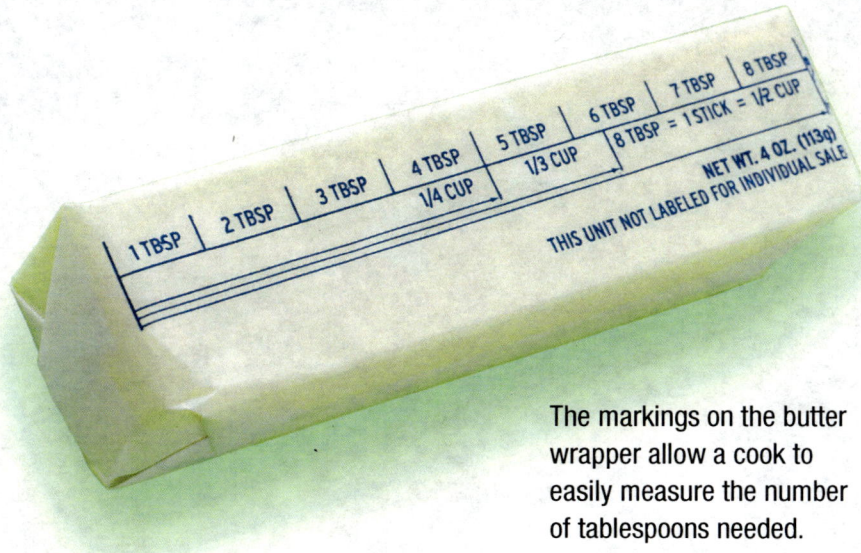

The markings on the butter wrapper allow a cook to easily measure the number of tablespoons needed.

a measurement of tablespoons? Before this confusion can **exact** too much stress, Zach looks at the wrapper around the butter. He sees marks that are labeled tablespoons. He counts off six marks and slices the stick. In the future, he will remember that a quarter-pound stick of butter has eight tablespoons.

Once the cake batter is done, Zach gets out the cake pans. The recipe says he needs two 9" round pans, but he only has 8" round pans. Zach wonders how much the size will **affect** the outcome. He knows baking requires precision. Zach finally decides this difference will not matter much as long as he tests the cake's doneness as the recipe says. Our cook has made another good decision!

VOCABULARY

source (SOHRS) *n.* person, book, or document that supplies you with information

exact (eg ZAKT) *v.* demand with force or authority

affect (uh FEKT) *v.* do something that produces an effect or change in someone or something

Famous chef Wolfgang Puck shows the appetizers he has prepared for a special dinner.

Once everything is ready, Zach breathes a sigh of relief. Now, how will it taste?

Zach's **achievement** as a cook is clear. His family members show their delight with the meal. Now he feels that there is no **limit** to what he might try next in the kitchen. He has good information and the right tools. He has a cool head when there are problems. Who knows, Zach might just become the next famous chef!

Discussion Questions

1. What might be the problem with each of these ingredient measures if they were listed in a cookbook?
   a lump of butter the size of a duck's egg
   a teacup full of vinegar
   a slice of liver the size of your hand

2. Cookbooks can be sources of information beyond recipes. What type of information would you like to find in a cookbook? What could help you when you run into an issue while cooking?

3. Is there anything in the modern world that you think would benefit from standardization? What is it, and how would you standardize it?

VOCABULARY

achievement (uh CHEEV muhnt) *n.* something important that you succeed in doing by your own efforts

limit (LIM it) *n.* the point, line, or edge where something ends or must end; boundary

Glossary

achievement (uh CHEEV muhnt) *n.* something important that
you succeed in doing by your own efforts **19, 48, 75**

affect (uh FEKT) *v.* do something that produces an effect or
change in someone or something **13, 48, 73**

benefit (BEN uh fit) *v.* bring advantages to someone or improve
their lives in some way **46, 70**

bias (BY uhs) *n.* an opinion about whether a person, group, or
idea is good or bad, that influences how you deal with it **46**

community (kuh MYOO nuh tee) *n.* group of people living
together; people united by a common problem or interest **44**

confront (kuhn FRONT) *v.* deal with something very difficult or
bad in a brave and determined way; accuse someone of doing
something by showing them proof **55**

contend (kuhn TEND) *v.* compete against someone in order to
gain something; claim to be a fact **50**

contribute (kuhn TRIB yoot) *v.* give money, help, or ideas to
something that other people are also involved in **37, 52**

cooperate (koh AHP uhr ayt) *v.* act or work together with
another or others for a common purpose **37, 47**

determine (dee TER muhn) *v.* decide; figure out **10, 25, 61**

direction (duh REK shuhn) *n.* general purpose or aim; the
general way in which someone or something changes or
develops **55**

distinguish (di STING wish) *v.* recognize or understand the
difference between two similar things or people **25**

diverse (duh VERS) *adj.* various; with different
characteristics **31, 59**

embedded (em BED uhd) *adj.* firmly fixed in surrounding
material **14**

enable (en AY buhl) *v.* give someone what they need to be able to do something **29, 42, 67**

enrich (en RICH) *v.* improve the quality of something, especially by adding things to it **37, 48, 68**

essential (uh SEN shuhl) *adj.* basic; necessary **20, 40, 69**

establish (uh STAB lish) *v.* make sure of; determine; set up **44, 62**

evoke (ee VOHK) *v.* produce a strong feeling or memory in someone **36, 71**

evolved (ee VAHLVD) *v.* grew gradually; developed **61**

exact (eg ZAKT) *v.* demand with force or authority **73**

examine (eg ZAM uhn) *v.* look at something carefully in order to make a decision, find something, or check something **7**

focus (FOH kuhs) *n.* center of interest or attention **13**

hypothesize (hy PAHTH uh syz) *v.* propose an unproved theory to explain certain facts **37**

identify (eye DEN tuh fy) *v.* recognize; point out **11, 22, 48**

imitate (IM i tayt) *v.* copy; mimic **24, 52**

immense (i MENS) *adj.* huge **5**

implement (IM pluh muhnt) *v.* begin to make a plan or a process happen **13**

influence (IN floo uhns) *n.* power to affect others **48**

integrate (IN tuh grayt) *v.* remove all barriers and allow access to all **48**

intent (in TENT) *n.* purpose; object; aim **7, 23, 60**

investigate (in VEST tuh gayt) *v.* try to find out the truth about something, such as a crime, an accident, or a scientific problem **6**

key (KEE) *adj.* important **30, 63**

limit (LIM it) *n.* the point, line, or edge where something ends or must end; boundary **75**

maintain (MAYN tayn) *v.* make something continue in the same way or at the same standard as before **44**

measure (MEZH uhr) *v.* find the size, length, or amount of something using standard units **59**

methods (METH udz) *n.* ways of doing something **13, 22, 46, 58**

narrow (NAR oh) *v.* decrease in width, extent, or scope; restrict **14**

participate (pahr TIS uh payt) *v.* take part in an activity or event **24**

persisted (puhr SIST id) *v.* refused to give up **9**

prevail (pree VAYL) *v.* gain the advantage or mastery; be victorious; triumph **57, 60**

prioritize (pry OHR uh tyz) *v.* put several jobs or problems in order of importance, so that you can deal with the most important ones first **18**

proceed (proh SEED) *v.* continue to do something that has already been started **14, 31**

purpose (PER puhs) *n.* intention; plan **33**

pursue (puhr SOO) *v.* continue doing an activity or trying to achieve something over a long period of time **9, 22, 70**

question (KWES chuhn) *v.* have doubts about something or tell someone about those doubts **6**

reference (REF uhr uhns) *n.* the act of looking at something for information; the book or magazine that you get the information from **69**

reinforce (ree in FOHRS) *v.* give support to an opinion, idea, or feeling, and make it stronger **20**

reside (ree ZYD) *v.* live in a particular place **27**

resolve (ri ZAHLV) *v.* find a satisfactory way of dealing with a problem or difficulty; settle **47, 71**

respond (ri SPAHND) *v.* react to something that has been said or done **36**

sensible (SEN suh buhl) *adj.* wise; intelligent **62**

significant (sig NIF uh kuhnt) *adj.* important **8, 29, 46**

source (SOHRS) *n.* person, book, or document that supplies you with information **72**

strategy (STRAT uh jee) *n.* plan for a specific outcome **12, 43**

study (STUD ee) *v.* apply your mind to; try to learn or understand by reading or thinking **16, 38**

undertake (un der TAYK) *v.* take upon oneself; agree to do **6, 25**

utilize (YOO tuh lyz) *v.* put to use; use something for a particular purpose **6, 25, 64**

Photo Credits

Cover: Playboy Archive/CORBIS; **iii: t.** © Elms/StockFood; **iii: b.** © Charles Palek/Animals Animals; **4–5:** © Private Collection/© Look and Learn/The Bridgeman Art Library Nationality/copyright status: British/in copyright until 2046; **7:** © Museo Lazaro Galdiano, Madrid, Spain/Giraudon/The Bridgeman Art Library Nationality/copyright status: German/out of copyright; **8:** © Jonathan Blair/CORBIS; **10–11:** © The Art Archive/Bibliothèque des Arts Décoratifs Paris/Marc Charme; **12–13:** © Vince Streano/CORBIS; **14:** © Bettman/CORBIS; **15:** Plaster reproduction of an inhabitant who died during the eruption of Vesuvius in 79 AD (photo) © Museo Vesuviano, Pompeii, Italy/Index/The Bridgeman Art Library Nationality/copyright status: copyright unknown; **16–17:** © Scala/Art Resource, NY; **18–19:** © Sean Sexton/CORBIS; **20:** © BL Images Ltd/Alamy; **20: t.** © William Leaman/Alamy; **20: m.** © William Leaman/Alamy; **20: b.** © Richard Day/Animals Animals-Earth Scenes; **20: bkgrd.** © David Muench/CORBIS; **23:** © Lisa Dumont/Alamy; **24–25:** © 2007 The Associated Press; **26–27:** © David Muench/CORBIS; **28: t.** © Richard Day/Animals Animals-Earth Scenes; **28–29:** © Joe McDonald/Animals Animals-Earth Scenes; **30–31:** © Charles Palek/Animals Animals- Earth Scenes; **32: t.** © Wally Bauman/Alamy; **32: b.** © Stouffer Productions/Animals Animals-Earth Scenes; **34–35:** © SuperStock/Alamy; **36:** © William Leaman/Alamy; **38:** © Peter Arnold, Inc./Alamy; **39:** © 2007 The Associated Press. All rights reserved; **40–41:** © Spencer Grant/Photo Edit; **42–43:** © 2007 The Associated Press. All rights reserved; **45:** © 2007 Photo Researchers, Inc. All Rights Reserved; **46:** © 2005 Getty Images; **48–49:** © 2007 The Associated Press. All rights reserved; **54:** © 2007 The Associated Press. All rights reserved; **56:** © 2007 The Associated Press. All rights reserved; **58: t.** © 2005 Getty Images; **58: b.** © Jackson/StockFood; **60:** © 2005 Getty Images; **61:** © Elms/StockFood; **62:** © 2006 AFP; **64–65:** © Rita Maas Studio, Inc./StockFood; **64:** © Richard Jung Photography/StockFood; **66: l.** © Brian Yarvin/Corbis; **66–67: r.** © Lew Robertson/StockFood; **67:** © Chris Collins/Corbis; **68: l.** © F. Hammond/photocuisine/Corbis; **68–69: r.** © Atlantide/Corbis; **70–71:** © David Young-Wolff/Photo-Edit; **73:** © Jupiterimages Corporation; **74–75:** © Fred Prouser/Reuters/Corbis